POEMS
From the
Heart

POETRY COMPILATION

Jackie Wiggins Payton and Iryah Banks

NEWMAN SPRINGS PUBLISHING
320 Broad Street
Red Bank, NJ 07701

First originally published by Newman Springs Publishing 2023

ISBN 979-8-88763-285-8 (Paperback)
ISBN 979-8-88763-286-5 (Digital)

Printed in the United States of America

This book is dedicated to my daddy, Arnesta Wiggins. It has been forty years since your death, and I still miss you dearly. Words cannot express the inspiration that you have always been in my life. Your unconditional love for me is always in my heart. This has been such a blessed accomplishment for me. I love you always, and always I love you. First and foremost, I would love to give thanks to the Most High, from whom all our blessings come. To my close family and friends, I would like to express my gratitude for your support in the working of our project.

I'd like to dedicate this book to my mom, who has always been the biggest influence in my life. And also to the rest of my family, who have always been there for me. I would also like to thank my elementary teacher, for believing in me and everybody else who I've come to know and love. Thank you.

Dedication: To My Daddy (Arnesta Wiggins)

To the man who meant the world to me.
I dedicate this letter from my heart.
I couldn't possibly begin to express just how much
You meant to me.
You were the first person whom I received
Love from, and in return, you were my everything.
At the time when you were raising me,
It wasn't common for a man to be
A single parent in the 1960s, but you
Were that for me.
From the bottom of my heart,
I can't thank you enough.
We were not the traditional family unit,
But we were in ever since of the word a family.
You did everything my friend's mothers did
For their families, cooked, cleaned, washed.
Made sure I was good.
I was only a few months old when you became
The sole parent, and that was a lot.
I'm blessed that you kept me and raised me
For eighteen years.
He always said if the Lord would
Let me live until you turn eighteen.
And that was exactly what happened.
Three months after my birthday, he passed.

It was devastating and very hard.
It took years to heal from his death,
But I finally got better.
I can honestly say that I turned out okay.
Never went to jail or got hooked on drugs.
So I feel like he would be proud of me
For following my dream of writing.
After all, I got it from him.

Love always,
Your daughter, Jackie.

He'll Make a Way

He'll make a way out of no way,
He'll open doors that have been closed,
All you have to do is stay faithful,
And continue to pray,
He won't ever turn his back on you,
He'll guide your path in the direction,
You should go,
Open your heart and give it to him,
And he will do the rest to keep you blessed.

—Jackie Wiggins Payton

Always

Always be thankful when he is guiding you,
He'll always be there to see you through,
No matter the ups or downs we endure,
We must trust in him from the start,
Always have him in your heart,
With life come struggles to make you strong,
Don't give up, don't give in,
This is a race you will win,
Because you are more than a conqueror,
You belong to the King.

—Jackie Wiggins Payton

Faith

There is no getting through life without faith,
Every day we wake up, we should always
Thank our Most High for breath,
We should do the best that we can,
He will do the rest.
No matter the problems big or small,
Just have faith, it will conquer them all,
Without a doubt I know for sure,
Faith gives you strength for you to endure,
Everything in life and much, much more.
Just keep your faith.

—Jackie Wiggins Payton

He Is in Control

Our heavenly Father is in control,
Has control, and will control all,
Nothing is done without his permission,
We need not be dismayed or confused,
Stay strong, praise him for his grace,
Praise him for his mercy,
And give him all the glory.

—Jackie Wiggins Payton

Trust

Trust in him that no matter what life brings,
You will always be a winner,
Trust that when it feels like no one is there,
He always is,
Trust that he has your back no matter what,
Look at yourself and your life
And trust in him that it will all be all right.

—Jackie Wiggins Payton

Strength

He is my rock and my strength
He holds me up and will never let me down,
Whenever I feel myself feeling low, to him in prayer will
    I go,
Nothing is too big for him, for he is mighty,
Just know whatever you need
You will find it all in him indeed,
He has the power to do anything
And everything in our lives for the better,
He is our sunshine in the stormy weather.

—Jackie Wiggins Payton

Thank You, Lord

Thank you, Lord, for my life
In having the chance to be a mother and a wife,
Thank you, Lord, for the life I live
And for having so much love to give,
Thank you, Lord, for touching my heart
And giving me a chance for a brand-new start,
Thank you, Lord, for all that you've done,
For creating the earth, moon, and sun
For the birds and the trees,
The flowers and the bees,
For the food that we eat,
And the water that we drink,
Thank you so much for everything that you've done
But most of all, Lord,
Thank you for loving us all like one.

—Jackie Wiggins Payton

Content

We need to be content in all that we might go through,
Be content in all that you do,
One thing we need to always do is not complain,
Because our circumstances will change,
They won't stay the same.

—Jackie Wiggins Payton

All We Can Do

All we can do is hold on tight to you,
Keep our life in your hands,
Only you can heal the land,
We just need to follow you,
And that's all we can do.

—Jackie Wiggins Payton

Fear not

Fear not, he will strengthen you,
He will daily feed us with his words of wisdom,
If we would only have an ear to hear,
And let him guide you with his eyes,
Get close to him while he is near,
So you won't have a reason to fear,
Fear not...

—Jackie Wiggins Payton

Just Know

I know that it seems like the world is on your shoulders,
When one problem ends, another one starts over,
But remember your faith is stronger,
Because you have Yah in your corner,
He's always by your side,
And he's always there for us with his arms open wide.

—Jackie Wiggins Payton

Tomorrow is not Promised

Tomorrow is not promised,
not even the next day,
We know not the time of our departure,
All we can do is just live
every second, every minute,and every hour one day at a time,
It doesn't matter how young or old with death,
It will eventually visit all of us one day,
But while we still have a chance
Always, always Honor our Heavenly Father,
Pray and do all we can to love our families and close friends
who are like our extended family,
Oftentimes we don't have as much time as we think to fix
        relationships or get yourself on a better path,
That's why we should definitely get out houses in order,
You can for sure be here today
and gone today,
Tomorrow is not promised.

Have

Sometimes, if we just sit and think about the things
we do have
Instead of the things we don't have,
We could see just how much we truly have.
To have the use of our minds is very powerful.
We can accomplish anything.

—Jackie Wiggins Payton

Time Is Winding Down

Time is winding down,
all we have to do is just look around,
So much chaos every second in a day
One side of the world is on fire
the other side is flooded with water, being swept away,
Much of life is being lost,
And all these comes at a very high cost,
The world is spinning and spinning around,
Time is winding down,
A lot of hate is being spread around like the evil
spirit it is,
People continue to do wrong instead of right,
They follow darkness instead of the light,
Each and every one of us has a choice to make,
It's up to us which direction we will take,
Time is winding
       D
         O
           W
             N

—Jackie Wiggins Payton

Emotional

Some days, I just feel like crying.
It hurts so much inside until it feels like I'm dying,
Other days, I'm happy, and a smile stays on my face,
I think about all the good times
And the laughter that took place,
And some days, I feel a combination of the emotions,
But all these feelings make up the emotional phase,
We have to go through the tough times
In order to enjoy the blessings made.

—Jackie Wiggins Payton

Stressing

Stressing over you.
Stressing over me.
Stressing over everything is how it is to be.
Things are wrong.
Things are right, but that doesn't keep me from tossing at
    night.
I can't shut down all the thoughts that are coming from
    my head.
Sometimes, I wish that I was somebody else instead, but in
    the end, I've learned to pray.
And put my burdens away and give them over to my
    leaning shoulder *the Lord*.

—Jackie Wiggins Payton

Gone but not forgotten

Your gone but not forgotten,
I miss you very much,
I think about you often,
I still remember your voice,
It saddens me that your no longer here,
But my heart holds you oh so near,
I miss the talks we had
Not to mention all the laughs,
We had a lot of good times
with memories that will always last
But most of all I miss your
warm and loving hugs,
and all the love you gave,
That always made me feel better it would put a smile on
    my face,
Your gone but not forgotten,
No one could ever take your place,
I will always Love you. ♡

This is dedicated to all of the loved ones we have lost.

I'm No Longer Here

I'm no longer here, where you left me to die,
You walked away from me, and I didn't know why,
It doesn't matter now,
I'll make it somehow,
Because my Father looks down,
He's high in the sky,
So go on to the thing that you want the most,
I'm staying right here to keep God ever so close,
He'll never leave me or forsake me,
This I know to be true,
He'll stand all around me because he loves me the most.

—Jackie Wiggins Payton

Getting Away

It's amazing how a trip to visit a close friend
can make you feel so much better.
A peaceful ride on a country road can ease your mind.
Change in environment, neighborhood, and city
Seem to soothe the soul.
Good company and long conversations,
plus, laughter can make all the difference in the world.
It's good to get away sometimes.
It changes your whole mood.
Just a weekend can do the job.
Thank God for good friends,
for without them it would be hard
to deal with all the pressures of life's problems.
Just having a smile or a kind word spoken to you,
Can touch your heart,
Especially when things don't seem to go your way.
Just know that it can all be better tomorrow.

—Jackie Wiggins Payton

Friends

Thank God for good friends
They'll stick with you through thick and thin,
Many times, I've needed your ears to listen to my problems,
By the end of the conversation
You had helped me to solve them,
Friends are dear to your heart,
Their friendship will hopefully never fall apart
I'm so fortunate to have friends like I do,
What would I ever do without you?

—Jackie Wiggins Payton

Time Is Precious

Time is precious every day that we have,
You should use it wisely,
Try to help someone along the way,
Sometimes, a smile can brighten a day,
Or a simple hello,
hope you have a blessed day,
Little things can go a long way
If we take a moment to do them,
You never know who is going
through a difficult situation,
Just remember, time is precious
And we should always keep this
as motivation.

—Jackie Wiggins Payton.

The Good Ole Days

I remember back in the days when me and my friends
    would have fun,
Running, jumping, and climbing trees
Playing hide and go seek, jacks, and hopscotch were
All the fun games to me,
Riding my bike was my favorite of all
Even though I had a lot of falls,
Life was so good without a worry in the world,
I had so many good times when I was a little girl,
These were the good ole days.

—Jackie Wiggins Payton

Moonlight

Shinning in the sky so bright
It can take your breath away,
It makes you wish that night would always stay
You've warmed many of my nights as I watched
High in the sky,
Glad to know that you're always there and
Always will be,
To brighten even the darkest nights
You'll always be special to me.

—Jackie Wiggins Payton

Thunderstorm

The smell of rain is in the air,
The sky is gray and cloudy,
Wind starts to blow and begins to get gusty,
Lightning lights up the skies as beautiful as can be,
I love the way it comes together so naturally,
The thunder starts to rumble, it shakes
the windows in the house,
The air has gotten cooler to let you know it's on the way,
A thunderstorm has formed, and it stays
For the whole day,
It's such a wonderful sight to see,
How beautiful a thunderstorm can be.

—Jackie Wiggins Payton

Spring Day

Flowers blooming and bird's chirping
On such a breezy beautiful day,
Winter is ending, and spring is on the way,
Butterflies and bees are flying all around,
As bugs are crawling on the ground,
It sure has been a wonderful spring day.

—Jackie Wiggins Payton

Snowy Day

Today has started snowing
It was such a beautiful sight to see,
I love to watch it falling; it's like a winter wonderland to me,
The flakes are all different; each one of them are unique,
I hoped that we would get some snow
It's been years since we did
Whenever it comes, it makes me feel like a kid
It takes me back many years
When I wanted to play and have
Some fun on a snowy day.

—Jackie Wiggins Payton

The World

Just sitting, thinking about how
different this world has become
nothing is the same,
All the sickness, death, and
Uncertainty that is in the world is not a game,
Even though all this is going on at one time,
Our Most High still has control, and soon it will be all fine,
We just have to pray and keep the faith and stay in the race
He will take care of us no matter what,
He does it with love and grace.

—Jackie Wiggins Payton

A Day in School

A day in school is kids screaming in your ear day after day.
A day in school is the teacher blabbering on in a classroom
while kids act up and throw paper airplanes.
A day in school tires you out, but you must hope that the
next day is better than the last.

—Iryah Banks

Clumsy Me

I titter.
I totter.
I completely missmoter.
Opps clumsy me.
I fanzel.
I danzel.
Opps clumsy me.
I *woosh.*
I wajsh then I fall.
One by one all in a line just like dominos we knock each
    other over. Not knowing who started it all, Oppsy
    doodle, *clumsy me.*

—Iryah Banks

Fear

Fear is clear in your eyes.
Fear is near and coming soon.
But don't fear cause the Lord made you, and he will keep
  you safe.

—Iryah Banks

Freedom

Being free, feeling the freedom is like a happy bird.
Being free is the best way to live life.
The best way to rejoice.
Being free is the way I want to live my life.
Being free is the way I want to live in this crazy world.
Being free in life is the way to be, so don't ever take precious
    life likely.

—Iryah Banks

Happy Day

Today was a happy day; let me tell you what I've done today.
Today I got a new car.
Today I bought a new ball.
Today I learned a new game, and all I did was win.
Then I went out to eat to celebrate my victory; yes, today
      was a happy day.

—Iryah Banks

Horrible Day

Today was a horrible day. A kid got gum stuck in my hair,
    and I can't get it out.
Today was a horrible day. I fell in the mud, and everybody
    saw laughed too.
Today was a horrible day. I got an F on a test, and you can
    surely guess that my mom was not thrilled at all.
Today was just a horrible day.

—Iryah Banks

I am...anybody I want to be. Nobody can tell me otherwise.
I am...my own woman.
I am...going to be a vet.
I am...going to rule the world one day.

Yes, I can. I *will*, and you can too if you just try.

—Iryah Banks

I Still Have Love For You

You may make me angry at times, but I still have love for
you.
You may make me feel sad at times, but I still have love
for you.
You may make me lots of ways, but this is the way we were
all made, and I want you to know that I will always
have love for you.

—Iryah Banks

I'm Blessed For

I'm blessed for waking up today because many have not.
I'm blessed to have food on the table because many are
    starving and dying today.
I'm blessed for a loving family that went through an awful
    lot to prepare and bring me here.
I'm blessed for all I am, and who I hope to be, and you
    should too, just like me.

—Iryah Banks

I'm Still Here!

The world may be going crazy, but…*I'm still here.*
The people are turning mean, and sneaky, but…*I'm still here.*
The world is ending, but…*I'm still here.*
So be there today and every day.
Be there for those who admire, love, and feel good in your presence.
Now be there to love, cry, laugh with the ones you love, need, and know.
Be there now, today, and forever.
And be proud to say…*I'm still here.*

—Iryah Banks

Listen

Here the birds singing a tune.
Listen, listen, listen.
Here the kids laugh and play a block away.
Listen, listen, listen.
Here the girl sings as she gleams.
Listen, listen, listen.
Listen to the sounds all around; just remember to always cherish, and remember these wonderful moments because they only last a second but live on forever.

—Iryah Banks

love's in the Air

You know that when Valentine's Day comes around that
    love is in the air.
When Valentine's Day cards start flying, you know that
    love is in the air.
When kisses and *X*s with lips appear, you know
That surely love was in the air, but has it always been that
    way?
It's just that when Valentine's Day comes around it's when
    it really gets to go
and shine.
PS: Happy Valentine's Day, everyone.

—Iryah banks

Pool Day

Slash, *wee*, *yah* today is a pool day.
Wow, *woosh*, *splash*, watch out. Here I come sling.
Ccccaaaa…booom.
Cccaaaa…bang.
Watch out below that was so much fun.
I can't wait to do it all over again next weekend.

—Iryah Banks

Sunshine

You are my sunshine.
Your smile can change the world.
It will turn all frowns upside down, so don't worry about
    a thing cause your smile will keep all bad Things out
    of your way.

—Iryah Banks

Colors of the Rainbow

Red: makes me feel like fire rising up in me.
Orange: makes me feel confused and weird.
Yellow: makes me feel rays of sunshine in my heart.
Green: makes me feel sick, and vomity down to the deep,
 dark, downright middle of my stomach.
Blue: makes me feel sad and lonely.
Purple: makes me feel calm and Zen.
Violet: makes me think of my mom and the rest of my
 wonderful family.

—Iryah Banks

The Heart Will Go On

You may feel sad, but the heart will go on.
You may feel lonely, but the heart will go on.
You may feel angry, but the heart will go on.
You can feel happy the heart will surely go on.
You can feel many different types of ways, but you can
always count on the fact that the heart will go on.

—Iryah Banks

Count the Stars

All one by one, there is no star more no less.
Each star has its own sunshine, but
You know that when one star burns out, another star will
shine in its place.

—Iryah Banks

What I'm Thankful For

I am thankful for *life*! A precious thing that can never be
    replaced.
I am thankful for *love*! A beautiful thing that is wonderful.
I am *thankful* for the things that the Lord has blessed us
    with, and I'm so wonderfully thankful for it all.

—Iryah banks

Family is the love you feel with the ones that you love.
Family is that warm feeling you get when the ones you
     love give you a hug.
Family is the love and warmth you feel when you get to
     wake up every morning to a familiar face at your side.

—Iryah Banks

World in Black and White

The world is changing; look around.
People are too; they now all mope around.
So try not to change, for there is nothing to be sad about.
For you are alive and well, but you cannot always say the
    same for the other.
So try to see the world in color.
For always try to look on the bright side, and try not to
    just see the world in Black and White.

—Iryah Banks

Dedicated to My Wonderful, Glorious
Mother, Jaterika Payton.

Your love inspired me to love others.
Your love taught me to care for others.
Your love and courage shines through the light.
You always find a way to brighten someone else's day.
  I love you for that, and I hope that you never change.

To mother, from daughter.

—Iryah Banks

A Boring Day

Today was a boring day. I woke up to a pony serving me
  soup.
Today was a boring day. I found a baby alien in my dad's
  suit before work.
Today was a boring day my teacher turned into an elf and
  the kids and me took over the classroom.
Yes, today was a very boring day.

—Iryah Banks

Iryah

Iryah Banks was born in Central Texas. At twelve and a half years old, in the seventh grade at Wellborn Middle School, Banks is the coauthor of the book *Poems from the Heart*, an AVID student, a Warhawks basketball player, a choir member, and a member of the Boys and Girls Club of College Station, which she has attended for over five years. The journey of creating and being part of this book began at the age of ten and has been an amazing experience. Banks hopes that readers will enjoy the book as much as she has.

Jackie Wiggins Payton was born in Central Texas. She received her education at College Station schools. After high school, she began working at a facility for the elderly, where she found the work to be very rewarding, and it held a special place in her heart. Jackie attended Blinn College to become a CNA, and she has also done home health work. She later returned to Blinn College for phlebotomy training.

Jackie has worked as a substitute for BISD and assisted with autistic children for a short time. At the age of thirteen, she started writing about her feelings and things she did day to day, which turned into a diary. A high school teacher first suggested that she should consider becoming a writer someday. She continued writing for the last forty-plus years but only for herself. However, in the back of her mind, she considered maybe doing something with her poems.

Family members and close friends urged her to give it a try someday. After all, it is a blessed gift. That day finally came when she decided to pursue it. Jackie has also been a gardener for the last four years, finding peace in both gardening and writing. She wants to encourage anyone who has a dream to step out in faith. You never know what you can accomplish.